"*The Winning Formula* is a game changer, I was blown away with the knowledge I gained from this book. I am now more than equip to catch the interest of C level executives and keep their interest which is the most important part. I highly recommend!"

— *Wendell H.* —

"I learned techniques in this book that I would have never thought of on my own! Prospecting is very hard but thanks to *The Winning Formula* I've got skills to snag their attention from the first call, email or hand shake."

— *S. Taylor* —

"...Mark shared this book with me as a reminder that even the sharpest tools need reshaping to adapt to changes. The insights on *The Winning Formula* depicts the daily conversations we have that enables even the novice of sales communicate in the most basic way: asking. The practice of repetition forms habit, and this book captures thru its chapters - a guidebook so to speak. As a colleague and friend, I thank Mark for sharing me this book that captures the common sense of good corporate communication."

— *Jay Pena* —

"[*The Winning Formula*] guides sales professionals in building their own authentic and personalized way to connect with potential customers. Packed with practical and actionable advice, this is a book for all sales executives and managers that respect customers' and their own time."

— *Pamela Valentine* —

The Winning Formula

The fastest, most effective techniques to engage 'C' level executives and decision makers through social medial, email and phone

Mark Ghaderi

ISBN-13: 978-1523687558
ISBN-10: 152368755X

Because of the dynamic nature of the Internet, any web addresses or links contained in this book may have changed since publication and may no longer be valid. The views expressed in this work are solely those of the author and do not necessarily reflect the views of the publisher, and the publisher hereby disclaims any responsibility for them.

A note on sources:
Since many of the sources I have used are online and I want to minimize the number of printed pages the bibliography and information on sources of data used have been placed online and are available by going to the following link: (www.thewinningformulabook.com/booksources)

Print information available on the last page.

To order additional copies of this book, contact:
sales@thewinningformulabook.com

*To my father with unwavering determination not to
settle for the path that was set out for him,
instead taking on unimaginable challenges and
hardships to ensure a better life for his family.
And to my mother for always putting her family first and
for always supporting her children in their endeavors.*

*I only hope that I could be half as good as you two
in raising my children.*

COMMUNITY MATTERS

As a member of my community I look forward to any opportunity to give back to my community in some small way. One of the charity organizations that I often support is the Special Olympics. As the Special Olympics organization puts it "This is a global movement that touches and changes lives for persons with intellectual disabilities through the transformative power of sports." Publishing this book gives me a great pleasure as I want to share my success with one of my favorite charities. I will be donating 30% of the proceeds from the sales of my book "Winning with Social Selling" to the Special Olympics of Singapore.

Rest assured that you not only personally benefit by buying (and reading) this book, you also help to support a worthy cause that brings joy to an aspiring athlete and everyone around this remarkable and special member of our global community.

ACKNOWLEDGEMENTS

I would like to express my heartfelt appreciation and gratitude to a lot of people who have supported me in writing this book. Firstly, I like to thank my family for giving me their support and encouraging me to keep going, even though it took away from our family time at nights and weekends. I also want to thank my friends and colleagues who helped me shape and structure my thoughts and ideas around a very big topic, offered me on-going feedback and cheered me on.

I most certainly want to express my gratitude to the business leaders and sales professionals who have honored me by attending my sessions, sharing their stories, giving me feedback and allowing me the opportunity to learn from them.

CONTENTS

"Two rules in selling:
Rule #1: Your first year in selling you are not
a salesperson; you are a prospector.

Rule #2: Every year is your first year in selling.

ABOUT THIS BOOK

First I want to say, "Thank you" and congratulate you for making the wise decision of buying this book that could improve your life by making you more successful as a sales professional. I also want to acknowledge that reading this book is the easy part. The hard part is executing the techniques shared and staying with it for at least thirty days to build the right habits.

Before you start, I want to set the stage and share with you what my assumptions were in writing this book and how you could maximize your return on the time you are investing in reading this book.

WHO SHOULD READ THIS BOOK

First I want to share with you the people and profiles that are best served by this book. The people who will benefit the most from reading and executing on this book are:

B2B (Business-to-Business) sales professionals who are looking for effective prospecting techniques that can double and triple their pipeline targeting the 'C' level executives and decision makers

Sales managers and leaders who manage sales teams, carry sales quotas, and want to double and triple their revenue.

Sales prospecting agents who are dedicated to identifying leads and handing qualified leads to their sales executives or clients and want to work smart, be happier with their work, build their career in selling, and in general, live more fulfilling and financially secured lives.

Why Did I Write this Book?

As a sales and marketing executive, consultant, enabler, and coach, I have seen numerous methodologies and techniques, and I have seen companies big and small spending millions of dollars and endless productive hours on sales prospecting programs and vendors that generate dismal results of around .05% to 2% success rate with unqualified and junk leads that cost thousands of dollars each. What often amazes me is that I see many sales leaders and managers have come to accept these dismal returns as acceptable. No! You should not accept 1% or 2% as an acceptable rate of return on sales prospecting.

First step in addressing this low return on investment is to ask ourselves, our reps, our vendors, and our sales leaders the question, "Do we know what sales prospecting really means and how we could improve the outcome?" As Einstein has said 'the definition of insanity is doing the same thing over and over again and expecting different results". Often times I think the way many sales executives prospect is insane, as they continue to do the same failure-prone cold reach and expect to get a better result.

It is time for us to treat prospecting as the very crucial and worthy cause that it is and empower our people with the right mindset and skills needed to succeed. Imagine how much more revenue you could have if you went from 1% or 2% success rate in prospecting to 15%-20%? That could be ten times more leads, ten times less contacts you need to make to get the same result, ten times more opportunities to talk to potential clients, and possibly 30% to 40% (if you use the 3X pipeline conversion rate) more revenue that you could be generating within weeks. How does that sound?

Well, if it sounds good to you then this book is your first step to getting there, and this is why I wrote this book.

Conventions Used in this Book

To make your reading more pleasant, I have used some conventions in the way I have marked up the book. There are points that I want to stress more and pitfalls that I want to warn you against. So here are the icons and symbols I have used to help you:

When you see *italic* words, it means these are example words and phrases I added to further clarify the point I am making. I have also used italics to mark up quotes from individuals.

This designates tips and tricks to make your life easier.

PROLOGUE

These days how do you start a conversation with someone you don't know? It's not easy, right? We all seem to be so busy and so preoccupied with our own issues, challenges, work, devices, etc. Now imagine how much harder it is to start a conversation about a new business, a business that starts by someone giving you some of their hard-earned money upfront in the hopes of you making their life better with your products and services. Now that's a difficult conversation to start, right? Well, that is what prospecting is all about -- getting someone to listen to you long enough to be interested to listen some more, with the endgame of making some kind of financial commitment.

Prospecting is really hard work, and it takes such tremendous amount of commitment, energy, and resilience that there are very few of us who could ever be great at it. Let me add that when I talk about being 'great' in prospecting, it does not mean that you win every time or even every other time. To be great at prospecting means going from 98% failure rate to around 75% failure rate. So this kind of success rate wouldn't get you into any Guinness Book of Records as far as I know. However, if you are an entrepreneur who just invested your whole savings to start a new venture and you have to build a customer base so that you could survive and grow, or a sales executive who wants to have a successful career beyond your wildest dreams and be financially secure, then going from a success rate of two out of 100 to twenty-five out of 100 is an amazing achievement.

WHY SHOULD YOU READ THIS BOOK?

Why does the world need another book on the topic of prospecting? Why should you spend your hard-earned money and your ever-shrinking hours and minutes to buy and read this book?

Well, the simple answer is because **the technique I introduce in this book works better than any other method or technique you may have seen or tried!**

Let me expand a bit more: When you are prospecting, you are fighting for the chance to influence someone's decision. The challenge of doing so in our over-crowded, super noisy, competitive, and cynical world is that many of your prospecting conversations will end within seconds, sometimes before you even start talking. Within minutes or even seconds, the prospect has already moved on and has lost interest in what you have to say. This is not necessarily because you don't have anything interesting to say. The reason is that oftentimes your approach has already put you in the same bucket with all the other product pushers, snake oil salesmen, take-the-money-and-run, and here-today-gone-tomorrow businesses that we have seen or heard about.

For my past twenty-plus years of prospecting, selling, and leading companies in dozens of countries and market segments, I have seen and tried some of the best and worst approaches to prospecting. For the past five years, I have been developing, teaching, coaching, and perfecting a prospecting technique that, executed properly, will improve your prospecting success rate by five times or more the average success rate!

I have delivered the Winning Formula workshop across multiple markets and have had sales manager and the sales executives be amazed by the success rate they could get using the formula. As part of my standard Winning Formula workshop I spend at least two days on site coaching the sales executives to help them get over the initial road bumps of learning a new technique. In every instance the clients have seen their prospecting success go from 1% to 2% to around 20% or more! A common response I get from a lot of sales people who try the Winning Formula for the first time is that they are surprised and often amazed how effective the technique is.

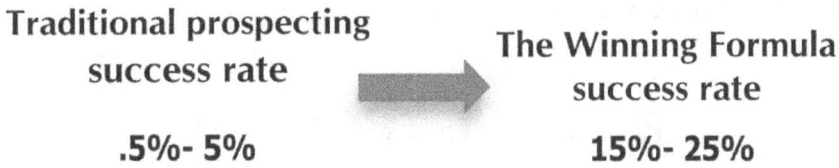

Traditional prospecting success rate

The Winning Formula success rate

.5%- 5%   **15%- 25%**

The best part about the Winning Formula technique is not because it is hard, super complicated, or difficult to master. The beauty of the Winning Formula is that it is very simple, clear and to the point, with little distraction from the main objective, which is to engage the decision makers.

So I ask you to read this book with an open mind; give the ideas the chance to take root, be honest about your current prospecting approach and consider if this approach could help you be more successful. I want to say upfront that I have been responsible for demand generation in three startup companies in multiple countries and worked in the small and medium companies, as well as large organizations with complex sales cycles and customer engagement models. But what I found to be common among all these businesses is that, at the end of the day, prospecting is about one person reaching to another person, trying to start a dialogue. Regardless of the company size, product, or complexity, it is about engaging and getting a buy-in from another person. This is a human interaction and will succeed or fail based on its ability to connect to the other party.

Being a big believer in social media and having written a successful social-selling book entitled *Winning with Social Selling*, I am going to share with you techniques and tools that will help your prospecting efforts by using telephone, email, and social media channels.

BUILDING THE HABIT

I, along with many of my colleagues who carry the torch of furthering the knowledge and skills of our fellow men and women, like to think that our superbly thought out and flawlessly delivered programs alone will make an individual or sales organization a world-class success. However, unfortunately, numerous studies have shown otherwise! These studies have shown that the actual training may count for only about 10% of the learning and internalization. The other 90% will come from learning by doing, learning from colleagues, and leveraging a work environment that encourages and supports putting to work what has been taught.

Companies spend billions of dollars a year to train their sales teams on products, methodologies, and techniques so that they become more productive. It is certainly a worthwhile cause, and it helps to pay the trainer fees and sell my books. However, this may only take you 10% of the way. How about the other 90% of the journey? To this end, there are two critical components that have to be in place before you can see the fruits of your enablement investment: front-line management support and immediate coaching to build the right habits.

Front-line management support

If the front-line manager does not support and encourage the implementation of the techniques, ideas and concepts learned, there is little chance that any enablement (or any other program for that matter) will stick. I have seen so many sales organizations where the leadership at some level decided that a certain program should be rolled out to the troops. Plans were made, people scheduled, investment made, facilitators and trainers flown in to run the training. Two or three months later, they saw little movement of the performance needle! Everyone was at a loss. Then you dig in a bit and find out that the sales manager(s) did not attend the training and/or believed in the program.

> *Imagine what would happen if a sales executive goes*
> *through a great enablement program and then returns*

to his/her desk with a new level of energy and enthusiasm, anxious to put to use what was learned but the direct manager would have none of it? I would say this kind of enablement, without explicit support and involvement of the front line mangers, is a total waste of time and money, not to mention wasting days and weeks of people's lives. Anytime I run a core sales enablement workshop such as the Winning Formula, I insist that the front-line managers attend the session as well. I also spend time with them to address some of the basics in coaching the sales executives on the techniques.

Immediate coaching to build the right habits

Success is a habit and not a single act. Effective sales prospecting is no different. To be good at the job, you have to build the right habits. The problem with habits is that they take time and repetition. This is especially hard to do with a new technique that may go against what someone has been doing for many years. That is why I recommend that post-enablement coaching should be part of some, if not all, sales skills trainings. In fact for some of the enablement programs that I have developed, including the Winning Formula, I schedule at least two days of coaching right after the workshop.

During the coaching days, I work with the attendees to get them through the initial road bumps to building the new habits. I have come to believe that this is extremely crucial in maximizing the Return On Investment of time and resources. I often have seen that in the absence of immediate support, sales executives fall back into their old habits.

To ensure the long-term success of the sales team, I work closely with the front line managers and share with them best practices on how to coach and mentor their sales executives.

The reason for having the coaching immediately after the workshop is the human brain's amazing feature to forget things almost as fast as it learns them. When you attend a training program, within a day you could forget almost 75% of the content delivered. Within a week you may only recall about 2% - 5% of the content. That is why I encourage you to put to practice what you learn immediately to improve retention.

Having said that, let's get started and make your next prospecting effort a new beginning that will define and propel you into becoming more successful than you ever imagined, with endless potential for future personal and financial growth.

"I have never worked a day in my life without selling. If I believe in something, I sell it, and I sell it hard."
— Estée Lauder

CHAPTER 1 — WHY PROSPECTING IS IMPORTANT

Anyone who has ever been in business, big or small, realizes the importance of having clients. After all, that is who pays for the bills, salaries, and keeping the lights on. But you cannot just hang on to a few customers for long. You need lots of clients to just keep the lights on. But if you want to grow and expand your business then the need for more and more new customers coming through the door or website is even greater. It's like the human blood cells. Your body has to keep making new blood cells to replace the old ones and to keep your body healthy and vibrant.

You need new customers to replace the ones that are bound to drop. It is the law of attrition. Customers change, come and go for various reasons that may have nothing to do with you or your products and services. Sometimes they go out of business, change people and priorities, stop and start activities that impact their engagement with you. So you cannot depend on a customer to be predictable. You need to lower the risk to your business by having more customers who could buy from you and support your dreams and aspirations.

We live in a very dynamic world where sometimes events taking place halfway across the globe can impact businesses, sometimes within weeks or even days. Your business needs to be well-diversified and supported by the marketplace so that you have more stability and resilience in coping with change. Think of what happened in 2008 with the world financial crisis. Millions of businesses around the globe saw the effect of the crisis within days and weeks. To live through such a crisis, you needed to keep your existing customers close and your new prospects even closer to ensure your survival.

Prospecting is also a great way for companies to listen and learn from their target customers. I cannot count how many times I learned about new products and new competitors when I was prospecting for new customers. It is a great market research tool that gives you direct, quick, and very honest feedback from your target market about you and your company. A few years back, while working at a startup in Seattle, Washington, while prospecting I heard about a company that apparently was offering similar solutions to what my company offered. This made me curious to research the company, and I quickly found out that the company was actually copying our service packages and selling it to the same market segment under a different name. After raising this issue with my boss, we figured out that we were pricing our services too low and were doing a bad job at marketing what we were doing. It really helped to re-evaluate our business model and improve our per-client revenue base. Prospecting is just pure gold as a market research tool.

Prospecting is a very personal form of marketing and advertising your business. You are making a personal connection with someone and sharing with them what you and your company are doing. I don't know how much more personal marketing can get. Prospecting done effectively is a great way to build your brand through the most powerful medium, word-of-mouth. Today with social media becoming the default channel for one-to-one engagement, you have the potential to build a brand that beats competitors thousands of times bigger than you by the way you use the medium and the message you share.

In today's hyperactive world, you and your business cannot stand still for long. You have only two choices, either change or be changed. Consider just the recent business giants that went from the dominators to becoming irrelevant. Consider Nokia, Kodak, MySpace, Blackberry, and the list goes on. The point is that the force of change is too great for any company to stay static for long. If you are happy with your business today and want to stay as you are, I am guessing that your competitors will not be happy with that setup. So for you to even stay steady, you have to constantly look for and recruit new clients in your current patch or segment, or go looking for clients in new patches and segments. That means you have to connect and engage with new prospects.

Another reason companies need to constantly prospect is the need to diversify. Imagine if you have certain products and services that are selling well within your target market. But due to external forces demand for your products may come under pressure and you have to look at diversifying and making new products. The Apple iPad is a great example of a company changing the rules of the game and forcing other companies to re-consider their product lines. We saw what happened back when Apple marketed its iPad for the first time. Suddenly a whole new market was created, and every PC and cell manufacturer was forced into making a product that they probably did not have before, tablets. In fact, some PC makers started to consider discontinue making PCs and only make tablets. When you make such a shift in your business, you have to go out and make new customers.

Doesn't matter if you are in a mature industry or the latest tech sector, without growing your market share, you have little chance for long-term growth and survival. You have to increase your slice of the pie or go after a other pies; it means you need to acquire new customers, which will mostly come from prospecting.

Now that we know we have to prospect for new clients let's start to look at what the job of prospecting really is and how to get better at it.

The number of sales calls it takes to close a sale
is determined more by your own belief system
than by the customer's willingness to buy.

CHAPTER 2 — CHALLENGES IN PROSPECTING

I think we can all agree that prospecting is hard work! It is one of the hardest parts of selling. It involves endless hours of contacting people who don't know you, getting rejected in multiple ways about 99% of the time, often not being treated with much kindness or respect, and usually getting little or no recognition from the company for the hard work. It is often a thankless job assigned to the less experienced and more junior staff in the company. No wonder nobody likes prospecting.

I have been teaching and coaching thousands of sales executives and demand generation agents, and I often ask the attendees at the beginning of my workshop to raise their hand if they like prospecting. I can count the number of people who honestly raised their hands in one hand. The question is, 'Why is prospecting hard?'

Here are some obvious reasons:

- It is all about rejection. With a success rate of around .5% - 5% (depending on whose stats you use), it means you are being rejected 99.5% to 95% the time. I am just guessing, but I don't think there are that many things that you continue to do if you are failing in them 99.5% of the times.

- It takes a lot of persistence to succeed. You have to stick with it for weeks, months, and years to get good at it. Most people treat prospecting as a junior position and will try to get out of it as soon as they can.

- Rejection is hard to take. It is hard not to take rejection personally. Doesn't matter how many times you tell yourself that it's not personal and they are just rejecting what you are selling and not you, it is still hard.

- You are going against human nature. When you are prospecting, you are asking the prospects to consider changing the way they are doing things. This by its definition is not something anyone likes to do willingly.

- There isn't a lot of good training available on the topic of prospecting. If you want to learn about selling, you could go to a bookstore or online and find thousands of books on the topic. But actually, if you start reading them, you'll find out that these books often start to teach you about selling once you have an opportunity in the pipeline, which is after the prospecting phase. I have done this simple exercise on Amazon.com, and it kind of aligns with the above observation. When I searched for books with the word 'SELLING' in the title, I got a hit of around 55,000. But when I searched for books with the word 'PROSPECTING' in the title, I got a hit of around 6,000.

- Prospecting is reaching for the unknown, which means you would be naturally out of your comfort zone, not knowing what to expect and how to react. It puts most people at a disadvantage.

- It is an unknown, and in the case of a call, it is an interruption from the recipient's point of view. So they are never ready for it -- just the fact that they don't know you will cause anxiety on the part of the recipient and will cause all kinds of defense mechanisms to kick in, which makes it harder to get through.

- The ever-shrinking attention span of human beings is making it so hard for us to be heard by the prospects. I am sure you have seen or heard that the attention span of people in recent years has gone to nanoseconds. This is just not enough time to connect and have a conversation.

"What we dwell on is who we become."
— Oprah Winfrey

CHAPTER 3 — HOW WE MAKE SALES PROSPECTING EVEN HARDER

There are many challenges in effective prospecting, and I already covered some of the reasons why prospecting is such a tough nut to crack. Now I am going to discuss some of the reasons why we as sales professionals and sales organizations make prospecting even harder than it is. I am going to talk about three ways we make our job even harder.

Wrong Assumptions

As sales prospectors, we make many wrong assumptions about the person they are calling. There are just too many wrong assumptions to go through all of them, but I want to highlight a few important ones that hamper our efforts in finding sales prospects from the first second of engagement:

The prospect cares about you, your name, and your company

Actually, no! They really don't care about you, who you are, your company, your sales quota, or whether or not you can feed your family. They didn't know you existed until they heard from you. So don't waste time explaining your title, your job, and all the other nonsense. More on this later.

If they don't show interest immediately, it means they don't need what I am selling

This is a major, self-defeating notion by many sales prospectors. It is perfectly natural to feel this way based on all of the "NO's" and "NOT INTERESTED's" you hear or the lack of response to your emails. But this is a wrong assumption. Let me ask you a question. If you contact a prospect a couple of times and you don't hear back from them, what do you think? You probably say, "They don't need my stuff," right? Well, studies have shown that you may be wrong!

The most likely reason why they didn't respond to you immediately or called you back is what I have tried to communicate so far, which is first, there is too much noise out there in the market and you are just getting drowned out and they are too busy to even know you exist. They didn't even see you, hear you, or read your message; you got buried under hundreds of other priorities. And second, even if they saw your message or heard your pitch, your approach/message was disconnected from their priorities and did not compel them to act. They forgot about you and your message almost as soon as you stopped talking as they moved to their next email, thought or conversation.

The message that I hope is getting through to you on this is that persistence is key to success in selling. This key ingredient of good selling has not changed since the beginning of time, and it is unlikely to change as long as there are buyers and sellers.

There have been a number of studies done that showed the majority of sales executives give up too quickly and that the majority of sales go to the person who does not give up on a prospect.

Mistake prospecting with product selling

You are not selling your product or services on a prospecting call. You are just selling the next step in the process. A big difference. I believe that a major reason for prospecting to have a success rate of 2% or less is that the sales executives confuse a prospecting call with a sales call, and within seconds of a prospecting call or right at the subject/title line in an email, they start to pitch products. DEAD WRONG! Let me give an example that I hope most people could relate to. When you meet someone you want to ask on a date, what do you do? Do you just start talking about how wonderful you are, or do you first try to get into a conversation? I think in most cases you will do the latter; you try to first have a conversation before you go for a 'close', right? This is the same when prospecting. Keep in mind that Prospecting call is not a sales call. It is just an opportunity for a dialogue, the chance to earn the right to have a longer conversation to see if you have enough things in common to carry the conversation forward; to go on a date, if you will.

Prospect is rejecting me personally

This is one of the big challenges in prospecting. You take the 'NOs' from prospects personally and they start to wear you down and make you mentally tired and demotivated. To take the high level of rejection, you need to separate yourself from your work and not see the rejection as a personal failure. There are a lot of techniques to use that will help you reduce the impact of hearing 'NO' on daily basis. Some high-level advice I give to my students and workshop attendees is to, first of all, start with a very positive attitude every day. Try to learn from every NO that you hear. Instead of focusing on the NO itself, focus on why they say it and when they say it. Are there days or times that you hear it more? Are there times that you experience less resistance depending on your attitude, tone of voice, level of confidence, message, etc.? This will help you to learn more about yourself and your prospect, as it makes the impact of the NO itself less stressful.

We Talk to the Wrong People

If you could just change this one variable, you will greatly improve your success rate in prospecting. I know it is not very scientific, but I am willing to bet that in well over 80% of the prospecting efforts, we are contacting the wrong person in the target companies. You may ask, "What do you mean by 'wrong' person?" My definition of the 'wrong' person in sales prospecting is talking to people who only have the power to say 'NO'.

Let me illustrate my point. If you are prospecting, by definition you are reaching out to the company for the first time (or reaching an existing client for a new opportunity), correct? So they don't know you, and they certainly don't have a budget set aside to buy your products and services; otherwise they would be talking to you and you wouldn't be making a cold call, correct? So if they have no budget for you think who in an organization can give you a budget that does not already exist? The answer is certainly someone at the executive or ownership level who has the authority to allocate a new budget. Therefore, by definition, if you talk to anyone outside of that level, you are talking to the wrong person because anyone outside of that category has no power to say, *"Yes, I like your product, and I am willing to allocate time/resource/budget."*

Wrong Message

Where do salespeople often get the content that they deliver to the prospect? Actually in most cases, which department is managing the demand generation teams?

Often the answer for the above question is the marketing department. What do you think is the primary focus of the marketing department? Of course, marketing does many things, but by definition the marketing department is responsible for successfully marketing the company's products. This product focus results in the marketing department's prospecting content to be more focused on the product and not the customer. It is only natural that when a conversation takes place between the buyer and seller, the seller is more comfortable talking about the product since that is what the seller knows best. When it comes to the marketing content, since the marketing department will have limited and often no direct contact with the customer, the messaging may not resonate with the prospects. Therefore, almost all of the messages you see or hear from sales prospectors are around what I have and what I can do, with little room to discuss the customer's needs and desires. Here are some typical sales prospecting calls and emails:

> *Hello, Mr./Ms. Xxxxx,*
> *This is Mark from XYZ Company. I am calling to tell you about our xxxx solution/product/services...*

> *Hi, xxxxx,*
> *This is Mark, and I am the account executive for your company. Do you have a few minute to spare for me to introduce my company and ...?*

> *Hi, xxxx,*
> *This is Mark from XYZ Company, and we are the biggest provider of xxxxx services/products, and I am calling to share with you our special offer for xxxxx. Would you be interested...?*

I think you agree the above examples are good representations of typical prospecting messages. I also think you would agree that from the prospect's point of view it is rarely the case that the above messaging would get the prospect excited about talking with the salesperson. Then if that is the case why do we continue to approach prospects with this kind of messaging and expect to get better results?

"We are what we repeatedly do.
Excellence then is not an act, but a habit."
— Aristotle

CHAPTER 4 – ANATOMY OF A PROSPECTING REACH

In this chapter we are going to look at a typical prospecting call, email, or social media message and see what are the common points of failure that plague 90%+ of our prospecting efforts. I will start by primarily discussing what common mistakes we make when we are looking to find new clients for our products and services. Then I discuss our major challenges in effectively starting a dialogue with our potential clients and how we go from bad to worse when it comes to developing our sales pipeline. I will walk through a typical prospecting message or call with its three phases: opening, main message, and closing while pointing out how we often fail to break through and engage with our prospects, resulting in such a high rate failure in our prospecting efforts.

THE CALL OPENING

Or in case of email or social media contact, the subject line and first line of the text.

One of the biggest mistakes that salespeople make is to start every contact with pre-announcement in loud speakers: **"Warning, warning, this is a sales call. Stop listening now. I repeat; this is a sales call with little value for you and your business. Stop listening."** We immediately announce to our audience that this is a sales call by everything we say and do. Here are some of the common call openings I have heard:

Hello, could I speak to Mr. John Smith?

Hello, this is Mark from ABC company. Is this Mr. Smith?

Hello, how are you doing today? ...

Good morning/Good afternoon, may I speak to John Smith please?

Good morning Mr. Smith. Could I have five minutes of your time?

Good afternoon, Ms. Jones. Is this a good time to talk?

Now, be honest and tell me, if you receive a call similar to these, who do you think is at the end of the line? Someone who is going to help you be more successful and achieve your dreams? Someone who cares about you? Probably not! He/she is certainly not someone that you know by the way they introduce themselves. It certainly is not a call you were expecting to get. So what options do you have left? The most likely option is someone who is trying to sell you something or someone who wants something from you, like the Internal Revenue Service, an unhappy client, or an unpaid vendor. I think you would agree that none of these sound good and not a call you will take with a lot of joy in your heart.

It is a pet peeve of mine when you have cold callers call me and start by asking, "How are you today?" or "How is your day?" Really? Do you really care about how I am doing? Is that why you called me, interrupting my day to ask me how I am doing? Is this what you get paid for? To call and see how strangers are doing? Well, my standard answer to that question is: *"I am glad you asked! I got a speeding ticket on my way to get to work, and I was late so my boss scolded me, and I just found out that my company is laying off half of its employees, …and yes, by the way, I just got my divorce papers in the mail. But I am doing GREAT. I am glad you called to ask me that."*

The point I am making is that we put ourselves at a major disadvantage when we start every call sounding like a salesperson. When we sound like a salesperson and the purpose of our call is to sell something, we almost **never** going to get a warm welcome. The reason I say that is because I have never met a person who likes to receive cold calls. I have asked this question in almost every Winning Formula workshop I have run across the globe, and I have never heard the answer *'Yes'* from rooms full of salespeople and executives! So why is it that when we call someone for the first time, we start by sounding like a salesperson? Almost every word, sound, and gesture we make puts us into that category that screams out **"Stop listening; this is a sales call!"**

What Happens Next?

We have established that our opening already has warned the prospect about our intentions. Therefore, what we say after our introduction/opening is for the most part irrelevant because the prospect has already decided that this is not a fruitful conversation and he should stop listening. Ask yourself, if you are talking to someone and they are not listening, are you communicating? Of course not! In a sales prospecting call, the moment the prospect stops listening (within seconds of the call) the sales cycle has already ended, and the prospect has moved on.

After the initial introduction and opening is where the sales executive delivers his/her 'pitch' to the prospect with the hope of raising curiosity or piquing the interest of the prospect through sharing some remarkable or unique insight that will get the prospect to continue with the conversation. The challenge with this part of the prospecting call is that it is often all about the vendor and product without touching on the prospect's needs and desires. This may be natural because the seller probably knows very little about the prospect and cannot make many deep and personal statements about the potential customer.

After the initial call or email message opening the average sales people get unhinged and desperately try to hold on to the prospect's time by throwing every buzzword function, feature, and jargon they know. This futile attempt only validates the prospect's initial reaction that this is a typical sales call and of little business value for the user.

What I want to show you later is how to tailor your message to your audience in seconds and quickly gain their interest so that you could take the conversation to the next level.

The Close

The last part of the prospecting call is the closing where the salesperson is supposed to finish the call and have some kind of commitment from the prospect as the next action item. But as we have been walking through a typical prospecting call, we know that we have already lost a majority of our prospects within the first few seconds of the call, and we no longer control the call. A typical prospecting calls often goes south early on and the best outcome the sales executive could hope for is for the prospect to say something non-committal like, "We'll think about it." Or "Send us your information and we will contact you if we have a need." These responses are pretty much a polite way to say "Leave me alone." However, most sales reps interpret these comments as a "win," since the prospect didn't just outright say "NO." Unfortunately, we all know what happens next and how much time is wasted chasing ghost prospects.

CHAPTER 5 — AGAINST ALL ODDS!

In this chapter I am going to talk about what are the core habits that could make you more successful in selling and sales prospecting. Without having the right habits in place you may still have some success, but you probably will not be consistently as successful as you could be. Pick any professional sport and look at the top players or teams. Their long-term winning depends on hard work, constant search for improvement, and focus. It is about consistently having and demonstrating the right behaviors that brings about winning.

In this chapter I am also going to talk about your mindset and how you should program or reprogram your mind to be a winner. I read a very interesting article a while back talking about the Olympics athletes and the importance of their mental state in winning. The article talked about how at that level of athletic fitness and ability, the physical strength plays a small part in winning as most athletes are already well-trained and fit. However, the number that stuck in my head was that an

Olympics trainer said at that level, 90% of the winning depends on the athlete's state of mind and mental readiness to win. To succeed in such a highly competitive and stressful job as sales prospecting you have to be mentally ready and already decide in your mind that you WILL achieve your goals.

Let's start by talking about the behaviors that make you more successful in sales prospecting:

- Persistence
- Discipline
- Positive Attitude

PERSISTENCE

This should not be a surprise to anyone that success in anything in life, be it getting an education, buying your dream car, finding employment, or meeting the right partner in life, requires persistence. The more persistent you are, the more likely that you will win. One of the shared behaviors you will find in the most successful sales executives is their rock-solid commitment to achieve their goals that they set for themselves.

I used to have a sales manager years ago who was extremely persistent and hardly gave up on a prospect. I saw the difference that persistence made with a service client we had in Tokyo. We lost the account to a big competitor one year. One day I was complaining about losing that account and the impact on our revenue for the year. My sales manager said with confidence, "I will get the account back next year," and he did! Even though we had lost the account, the sales manager went to the customer about twice a month and kept in touch with the key contacts in the account. He continued to engage, listen, and learn more about the customer and how to win them back. Finally, with his persistence and single-mindedness, he got the account within a year!

Studies of successful prospecting have shown that the probability of winning over a client increases by the level of persistence by the sales executives. But I am willing to bet that most of us already have learned in the School of Life that if you want something you have to go after it and don't give up so easily. The more persistence you show, the more likely it is that you get that job/deal/degree/date that you are after.

When reaching any prospect, you must have at least four or five touches (contacts) before you give up and move on to the next prospect.

I am aware that some trainers and sales gurus advocate that you should never give up on a prospect and keep at it until you hear 'Yes'. Frankly in principal I agree that you never want to give up on a prospect. But the reality of life and our job as sales professionals is that we need to reach out to more and more prospects in order to build our pipeline. We are also given limited resources and time to achieve results. I also believe that you cannot serve every customer all the time. So if I am reaching a prospect five or six times using my best moves and I still cannot get traction, I am confident that there are other prospects out there that they really need my help and I prefer to spend my energy where it is more fruitful and appreciated.

DISCIPLINE

Long-term success in anything takes discipline day in and day out. Again, going back to the sports metaphor, have you heard of any successful athlete who practices and works out once in a while, without a set schedule, preplanned set of exercises and milestones? You won't because it is not possible to achieve that level of efficiency and results without following a well-planned set of activities. If you have ever managed any teams or projects and have dealt with a team with different levels of discipline and commitment, I am sure you have noticed that the people with more discipline are more likely to deliver results consistently and be more productive over others who lack discipline, regardless of how much smarter and more competent they are.

In sales prospecting discipline means setting up an activity schedule based on your business priorities, then sticking with it despite all the distractions that will happen around you. Most sales teams and companies I have known see prospecting and demand generation as something they do only when they run low on opportunities, or when there is an environmental shift that demands action such as a financial crisis, market shifts, or competition level. I have sales leaders shout out at their sales executives to go and build a pipeline because the pipeline looks bad for the week, month, or quarter. But as soon as a few new opportunities show up or the pressure is off, they cut back on prospecting. And the leaders then complain about performance inconsistency. Duh! This is the wrong approach.

You have to commit to demand generation no matter what. You have to set workable and effective prospecting objectives and activities that will become part of your DNA that does not change just because the pipeline looks "pretty good". Only then you will enjoy consistent and long-term success.

At an individual level this means having your day preplanned with set times to prepare for your prospecting time (the day before) and then executing your prospecting plan. You will be amazed at how things fall into place once you evaluate your priorities and set your daily and weekly activities accordingly. Without discipline, you are always at the mercy of the external forces to kick you around like a soccer ball. I always say 'drive or expect to be driven'. More on effective time management later.

POSITIVE ATTITUDE

Regardless of your skill set, natural talent, or years of experience, your attitude determines your success in life. I believe that it is impossible to be a successful sales professional if you don't have a positive attitude. Selling by definition is about having a positive attitude. Why would you even bother getting into a line of work with 90% + failure rate? When you are prospecting, it is particularly crucial for you to have a very positive attitude because first of all, you are often contacting people for the first time, and if you don't have the right attitude, there is little chance that they would want to talk with you. Why would they? Who would want to start a conversation with a stranger with a bad attitude? When you don't have the positive attitude it is transparent and it comes out in your voice, body language, and the words you use. People can feel and sense it, and they don't react positively to a negative approach.

Secondly, since the rejection rate in sales prospecting is so high, the high failure rate naturally sucks out your energy and enthusiasm. You have to come to work with an ocean full of positive energy that could supply you with the necessary energy and motivation to carry on the whole day.

One of my favorite quotes on the role of attitude in selling is from one of sales profession's Hall of Famers, Zig Ziglar: *"Your attitude, not your aptitude, will determine your altitude."*

MAKING THE MIND SHIFT

One of the first steps in becoming better at sales prospecting is to have a genuine and sincere mind shift on your approach to prospecting. I find it interesting that as a customer, we often complain about the cold calls we receive from other sales reps and how they waste our time and show no respect for our time. But once we put our hats on as the sales executive, we often behave like those irritating sales prospectors we complain about, and yet we expect the prospects we call to welcome us with open arms!

This is a simple but difficult shift, and it is about you putting yourself in your customer's shoes and thinking about how you would react when you are getting a cold call or prospecting email. I'd like you to read the following question and think about it for a few minutes before you continue reading:

If you are the customer/prospect, what do you want to hear from a salesperson to become interested in continuing the conversation/correspondence?

This simple shift will first make you more tentative and aware of the prospect's state of mind when he/she gets your email or call. Second, it helps you better tailor your tone, wording, body language, and message to the audience. Third, it will (or at least it should) make you ask the question, "Why should the prospect read my email or listen to me?" This question should get your wheels turning to find out why and how what you are selling will serve the prospect. Then you can build your message around your added values.

Acknowledge the elephant in the room

Let's face it, nobody likes being bothered by a cold call or prospecting email. But at the same time we have to accept that businesses need clients and revenue. In my opinion, there is little you can do to change the fact that you need to find new clients, and you have to start by reaching out and letting people know you are there. Knowing and acknowledging this fact, instead of fighting it, let's effectively leverage the cold-reach dynamics to achieve your goal in sales prospecting. Here are some elements of sales prospecting to keep in mind:

- Initially you may have little knowledge about the prospect and his/her interests/challenges and desires.
- The prospect didn't ask to be contacted, and therefore your reaching out is an unwanted interruption.

- You often have a very limited time (seconds) to generate interest and secure a follow-up action.

In chapter 7 I lay out my approach to prospecting and address how to turn these elements that seem to work against you to work for you, turning a cold reach into a prospecting engagement that aligns with the prospect's desires and interests. To this end I cannot stress enough the importance of social media and how you should leverage it whenever possible to build value. In my last book *Winning with Social Selling*, I discussed why and how you should build a solid social media presence and position yourself as a subject matter expert and valuable resource that your prospects should know and engage with.

"Until you contact the customer,
you haven't done anything."

CHAPTER 6 — LEARNING THE AIDA PRINCIPAL

The question around how to be more effective at sales prospecting is not new. Businesses and sales professionals have been dealing with this question for centuries. But one of the most effective models for answering this question has been around since 1898. It was developed by an advertising and sales pioneer, Elias St. Elmo Lewis, who was trying to figure out a better, easier way to sell. He came up with the model that is now known as the AIDA model. His model maps out the journey the sales professional should take with the prospect in order to get the desired result. AIDA explains the sequential steps a prospect will go through before taking action in a purchase.

Many books you pick on marketing or selling touches on AIDA and lend some credit to its validity. But what I have found is that often these books don't dig deeper into the model and how the sales person should leverage it to gain interest and insight.

Think of the AIDA this way. When you are reaching a new prospect for the first time your desire is for him/her to go from

"Who is this person?" or "What is this message?" to thinking/saying, "I want to hear more" or "I want to take the next step"

Let's get into what AIDA is and how it can help you be more successful.

Here is what the AIDA model means and why you should care:

Attention

Whenever you want to engage and influence someone, the first step is to make sure you have his/her attention. In the case of your prospects, when you contact them by email or phone or any other way, you first have to get their attention, because if you don't have their attention anything you say or do goes unnoticed.

If someone is talking to you and you are not listening, does it matter what they are saying? If someone is calling your cell and your cell phone is not receiving the signal, will you hear anything? The answer is NO. Whenever you want someone to take an action that you desire, doesn't matter who-- a prospect, your teenage son, your boss, or your spouse -- first you have to get their attention so that they are receiving your message. Again, once you call someone and you immediately position yourself as a salesperson, do you think they are still fully engaged and listening to you? More than likely the answer is NO! Most of the 95% - 99% sales prospecting failures happen at this first step, within the first few seconds of reading or hearing a salesperson's opening.

Interest

Once you have someone's attention, you are halfway there. Now they are listening or reading your message and hopefully understanding it. Your next job is to say something that will earn their interest and make them want to find out more. Here is where you need to think about what your prospect wants to hear and what will make them continue reading or not ending the call. Think about what every one of us care about the most. What is it that you care about the most? I would guess, as most people, you care about your family, your job, your money, your community, etc. In other words, you care about YOU and what is important to you more than anything else, right? So if someone wants to get your attention and interest, they need to say something that you care about.

You may say, "I don't know what my prospects care about." The answer is, you are right. You probably don't know exactly what someone cares about, but you can certainly make some good, educated guesses. Here again I want to emphasize the role the social media channels can play in helping you identify what people and businesses care about. For example, if you see someone is posting articles about the environment or supporting environmental causes, it is pretty safe he/she would be interested in environmentally friendly goods and services.

When it comes to b2b selling in some ways it is actually easier than b2c selling. This is because it is easier to answer the question "What does the business care about?" Here is why: When it comes to business executives, what do they care about the most? Of course, themselves, but in the context of their role, what they care about the most is their KPIs (Key Performance Indicators). This is a very critical element of effective prospecting.

One of the rules for effective prospecting is that you should know the KPI of the individual you are contacting. If you don't know it, don't contact them, period. Because in the absence of this information, your message is likely to fall on deaf ears. Also note that executive KPIs don't change very much from one industry or country to another.

That means that a CFO in the USA has pretty much the similar KPI of a CFO in Japan or the U.K. The reason is that most businesses in the world share similar interests in revenue, profit, margins, market share, competition, and innovation. I had a fairly junior sales executive in the Philippines once ask me to share the KPIs for a CFO in the Philippines vs. a CFO in North America. My answer was that because of the cultural and environmental variations, there may be subtle difference in the KPI numbers and the way they are measured, but I was certain that having good cash flow is just as important in either country.

In Chapter 7 I will cover the KPIs of key executive roles and how you should use them to customize your prospecting messages.

Desire

Once you have the prospect's interest, you are almost home as the prospect now would have the desire to continue his/her engagement with you. In a B2B selling, once your prospect is interested in what you are saying, then he will have the desire to continue to talk with you more, meet you, or reply to your message. Keep in mind that when you get to this stage, the level of interest and desire of the prospect depends greatly on your messaging and how the prospect perceives the value you bring.

Action

Only after you gain the interest of your prospects and they have the desire to continue engaging with you, they will be willing to take some form of action to continue the engagement. This action could be to continue talking with you, setting up a meeting, introducing you to someone else, or even placing an order. But the level, timing, and intensity of the action are more likely to be in direct correlation to the perceived value you have built for your product or service up to that point. In other words, you earn the right to ask for something based on how effective you have been in earning the prospect's interest. You cannot ask for access to the CEO of a company just because you said you have a great product.

"Change before you have to"
Jack Welch

CHAPTER 7 — THE WINNING FORMULA

In the next three chapters I will show you how to build a winning sales prospecting message (***Winning Pitch*** or **WP**) that will increase your success rate by as much as 500%. The formula is simple and easy to do. I assure you that the Winning Formula for sales prospecting is much easier, faster and more effective than many techniques out there. Not only that, my Winning Formula is also very scalable and re-usable. You don't have to spend hours researching clients, looking up companies and databases. Its effectiveness comes from its simplicity and structured approach following the AIDA model.

Having said that, I want to give you my disclaimer here. I have been around and done this long enough to know that there is no single silver bullet formula that will apply to every situation in every market. As they say, there is more than one way to skin a cat. I am not saying this is the only way to prospect. There are many other approaches that could work based on your market, industry or the target prospect. But if you want to dramatically increase the effectiveness, consistency and quality of your leads, then the Winning Formula is the way to go. If you are using a technique that gets you consistently 15% to 25% or more success rate in cold reach, then you stay with that. Consider *The Winning Formula* as another tool in your sales toolbox with a high level of success.

DON'T QUACK

Before we get into the technique itself, I want to share with you a basic principle of my Winning Formula. As the saying goes, *"If it looks like a duck, swims like a duck, quacks like a duck, then it probably is a duck."* Same goes with selling and salespeople. The biggest challenge in successful sales prospecting is that simply from the first moment we engage with the prospect, we act and sound like a salesperson. Therefore, we are treated like an uninvited and undesirable guest that that nobody wants to engage with.

A key principal of the Winning Formula approach is to simply **"stay outside the sales cycle."** What this means is that your prospect should not see you and your initial contact as a start of a sales cycle. Because once they realize that your primary value-add is to sell your product, their primary instinct is to push you away and end the sales cycle. It is important for you to understand the above point and take note that every touch point with your prospect/customer should be less of a sales meeting and more of a business support and value experience.

The Winning Formula: The formula has three simple and straightforward components:

1.   Opening (optional)
2.   Grabber ("About" or "For")
3.   The Ask

Opening

This is basically where you often introduce yourself or have what I call a soft landing. Most sales people feel that they have to have a typical introduction where they say or write their role, title, name, company name, and perhaps add a bit of conversation and chitchat.

Let's first look at the wrong way of doing this. Often sales reps start with a phrase like this:

> *"Good morning. This is Mark from ABC company. How are you today..."*

> *"Good afternoon. This is Mark, your account executive at ABC company, and I am calling today to tell you about a special..."*

> *"Hi, this is Mark from ABC company calling you to see if..."*

These kinds of openings are unnecessary and only hinder your efforts to gain access.

Every time I run my workshop, almost all the salespeople have this misplaced belief (perhaps carried over from past generations) that when prospecting for new clients it is important for the salesperson to take precious minutes and seconds to introduce himself or herself. This is especially true in more traditional cultures. I have had a lot of heated debates about this topic in countries such as India, Japan, Korea, Thailand...

But frankly, please accept the fact that your prospect in the context of his/her job at the beginning of talking to the stranger just **does not care who you are and where you are calling from.** They are listening for R&V (Relevance and Value). Think about it. Until you called them they didn't know you existed. Why would they care who you are? What they are thinking is "Why did you call me" and "What can you do for me", Period.

Let's go back to the AIDA model. As we said, you have to first get someone's attention before you can deliver your message. So the first few seconds of a prospecting call (or the subject line of an email) is very important to get the person's attention. Don't waste those very precious seconds on introducing yourself and announcing to the listener or reader that this is a prospecting touch and you just want their money. As I hope you got this message by now that most of us are not willing to part with our money, and even less willing to spend our time talking to salespeople who just want to take our money. Having said that, if you feel that without an opening you cannot move forward, then by all means, use one. However, make your opening very customer-focused, simple, non-technical, and as short as possible, keeping in mind that your opening may actually hurt your chance of success if not done well.

To clarify, I am not saying you hide who you are or where you are calling from. You certainly can reveal that information during your call. But you don't need to do it within the first few precious seconds of the call, causing the listener to get his/her anti-salesperson guards up. If the person likes your message he/she could and would certainly ask, 'Who is this?' or 'which company are you with?'

Key points to remember about introductions:

- Make them as short and simple as possible. Don't use complicated, hard-to-understand titles that makes people think, "What do you do?"

- Avoid saying the words in your title that boxes you into a category of people or department that will reduce your chance of success in engaging with the executive level. For example, if your company name or title says "cleaning services" or "software" or "training", then don't be surprised if you immediately get transferred to lower levels in the company where they have no power to allocate budget for you.

Again, given the choice, just skip the opening/introduction and go right to the next part of your message. If they like your Grabber, then you can always introduce yourself.

CHAPTER 8 — THE WINNING FORMULA: GRABBER

The Grabber is your key value that should get the prospect's attention and interest by talking to that person's business priorities (KPIs). Sometimes you call this your *sales pitch* or *elevator pitch*. If you are delivering the grabber in a call or in person, it pretty much contains the whole business value. In case of prospecting via email or social media the title/subject line, plus the first one or two sentences in the body of your email will constitute **the Grabber**.

The Grabber has to have the following:

- Has to be about the prospect and what he/she cares about. It is not about you or your company. This is not about your company history or products.

- Has to show value the prospect gets from you and your company. This could be sharing the past value you have delivered to other companies like them or to the same industry. Your value could be targeted towards that particular role or the company. For example, you can say how you helped people in the same role as the prospect's role or how you helped a company in the same city, industry, employee, or revenue size.

- Has to speak to the KPIs that the executive cares about. This means you have to define your business value in terms of that executive's KPI. For example, if you are selling office-cleaning supplies that disinfect surfaces and kills germs, then you should not call the CFO or facilities manager with the pitch that you are selling cleaning agents. Your pitch should be that you improve employee health and reduce sick leaves due to catching cold or flu. If you are selling software, you should not say you sell great software, because that will quickly route you to the IT department, which almost never has the power to give you money they don't have in the budget already.

- Must be delivered during the first thirty seconds of the conversation or email message. The key is to be quick, clear, and simple so that the prospect can understand enough to make a call whether to continue or not before he/she stops listening.

The Grabber could be:

- About your experience in helping others, preferably in similar profile as the prospect.

- Share new opportunity for the prospect to help them be more successful. For example, other companies are leveraging cloud technology to reduce cost; how about yours?

- Share a challenge(s) that the prospect's industry is facing and how you can help them. For example, the rising fuel cost is hurting logistics for companies like yours. We can help you better manage that cost.

- Interesting fact(s) about a relevant topic such as industry trends, governmental changes, relevant survey results, new ways to look at old problems, future trends, etc. For example, a customer survey showed that consumers will reduce spending on luxury items next year because of the new, higher consumption tax. Here are some ways you could keep the demand high.

Your Grabber may come in two forms:

1. About the prospect
2. For the prospect

1: About (the prospect)

What is the best way to get your friend's attention in a crowd? You probably shout out his/her name? How do you start to build rapport with people you just met? Probably talk about their interests and what they do, right? Of course you can't go around shouting out people's names. In a business email or call, one way to get their attention is to say something specific about them personally or about their company. Everybody likes to hear about themselves. A CEO or CFO of any company likes to hear people tell him/her what a great job he/she has done or how interesting his/her last blog or tweet was. So use this to get their attention and listen to you for a few seconds longer.

Here are some examples:

I saw your interesting blog on the topic XYZ and I am reaching you to...

I saw your press release about your new product and I'd like to share with you...

I saw in today's Business Review that your company is planning to open new offices in XYZ markets. We help...

2: For (the prospect)

With this approach you focus on your value delivered and get the attention of the prospect with how you could help them in their business. It is very simple and straightforward. You need to keep in mind that the value has to be relevant and talk directly to the job title you are contacting. You need to know the KPIs that your product will impact and then find the job title that has those KPIs as hot buttons.

USING A GRABBER FOR C-SUITE PROSPECTS

CFO

We work with many logistics companies like yours to reduce their fuel cost by as much as 22%. I would like to show you how we could help you achieve similar savings.

We help finance managers to improve Days Sales Outstanding by 14%.

Fortune 1000 CFOs are improving financial decision-making speed by up to 100% through using our market data services.

HR managers are reducing costs by 25% by outsourcing their payroll services to our company.

We help auto parts makers to decrease defects by 11%.

CMO/VP of Sales

We work with VPs of sales to increase sales pipeline by up to 78%.

We help sales leaders to increase customer satisfaction by 16% within three months.

Sales leaders in your industry increase sales productivity by up to 46%.

MORE ABOUT KPIS

Here is a good place to expand on the topic of KPIs and what they are for different titles. Since the focus of this book is selling to the executives, I am going to cover some of the top positions in companies. These could apply to small and medium companies as well as the large companies, keeping in mind that there could be some variations based on the industry and company structure.

Executive KPIs

Let's start from the top:

CEO's/owner's areas of interest

- Balanced Scorecards
- Returns – ROI, ROE, EPS
- Profitability %
- Sales Growth
- Strategic Planning
- Shareholder Value
- Share prices
- Brand value

CFO's areas of interest

- Returns – ROI, ROE, EPS
- Profitability %
- Cost of Capital
- Cash Flow
- Receivable (DSO)
- Budgeting & Planning

COO's areas of interest:

- Operating Margins
- COGS
- SG&A
- Asset Utilization
- Inventory
- Productivity Metrics

CMO's/Sales areas of interest:

- Market Share
- Service Levels
- Marketing Effectiveness
- Sales Pipeline
- Brand Value
- Average Deal Size
- Competitive Situation

So if you want to reach out to any of these titles, you need to speak to one or more of these KPIs. But remember that depending on the market, country, and the business environment, some may become more important than the others. For example, if you think about the financial crises of 2008-2009, days before the collapse of some of the world's largest financial companies, the priority of companies were different. But after the collapses, suddenly universally every 'C' level and executive's priority became just survival, and that meant cutting cost and maintaining top line.

The above is a short list and leaves out many job titles and KPIs. You as a sales executive need to spend an hour or two to identify what are the hot buttons for the job titles you are calling into. For example, if you are selling to the head of HR, you need to consider what does the HR head care about? It is safe to say that the HR head would care about employee recruiting, on-boarding, safety, training, etc.

In general, identifying relevant KPIs for most executive titles is not too difficult. In my Winning Formula workshop, we spend a fair amount of time to identify relevant KPIs for the attendees and do a lot of scenarios and role plays around various titles and how to quickly identify the right KPIs.

CHAPTER 9 — THE WINNING FORMULA — CALL TO ACTION

The right CTA is the one that you ask for what you want, directly and clearly. You then stop talking. Let me emphasize the last part: once you ask for what you want, you **"STOP TALKING."**

I could write about CTA for pages, but I try to keep my message as short as possible. This is often the final stage where the sales reps could hurt themselves, and unfortunately they often do; destroying all they have built by simply not having a good ASK, becoming nervous and not asking at all, or just stepping over themselves and killing their chances by talking and pitching too much. As I said in chapter 7, you have to stay outside the sales cycle so you are not treated like a salesperson, because once you are seen as a sales executive trying to just sell them something, they stop listening and then.... Remember the AIDA.

One of the common mistakes I see from sales executives is that they are not comfortable asking directly for what they want. It is understandable because they are worried about hearing a

'NO'. So instead, they often call without a clear goal or don't ask directly for what they want. This only causes more confusion and anxiety for the prospect on what to do and how to respond.

A poorly conceived and executed prospecting touch is where you reach a prospect without a clear objective and value proposition followed by an ambiguous closing and call to action where we often ask the prospect what they want to do. This is not a very effective way to achieve your goal in building a sales pipeline.

As I said in chapter 7, you want to stay outside the sales cycle by making sure that the engagement experience does not feel like a sales call. These are some of the common, and often wrong, "asks" I hear from salespeople:

> *"I'd like to meet with you to tell you about our products."*
>
> *"I'd like to introduce my company to you."*
>
> *"I'd like to introduce myself and my company."*
>
> *"I'd like to see if you have any need for XYZ products or services."*
>
> *"I'd like to ask if you are interested in signing up for our special introductory offer..."*

I think you'll agree that, first of all, the above 'ASKs' are all seller-centric. Secondly, they categorize you as a salesperson, which again, is something that often works against you.

Remember, firstly try to stay outside the sales cycle by asking for something that is different than what the other sales representatives ask for. Secondly, you want to ask for something that is not complicated and they don't have to think about it too much, keeping in mind that spending money they didn't budget for is not something they would be interested in doing right away. So what can you ask that does not put you in an awkward selling situation and keeps the person's interests in mind?

ASKING FOR AN APPOINTMENT

The purpose of prospecting is to find an interested party to listen and act on your recommendation. In other words, you are looking for an opportunity to influence others, which starts by having a two-way communication. As we discussed in chapter 6, you have to have their attention and interest before you can move them to the next phase of having a desire to work with you. This could only happen through a pre-scheduled time with a specific agenda and well-prepped discussion points and questions. So the best ASK you could have is a short in-person or remote meeting that will help you explore the possibility of having a win-win business engagement. You will be asking for a short meeting/call/video conference in the future (not now) to better understand the prospect and uncover needs so that you could properly qualify the lead.

One important point I mentioned above about your ASK for appointment is to be for a future date, not on the spot when you called, emailed or met the prospect. The natural question you may ask is "why don't I just keep talking and try to get more out of the executive and maybe sell him/her while I've got them?" This is the exact reason why you don't want to do so, because if you start to have that meeting immediately, you don't have enough knowledge about the prospect, and in the absence of that, you naturally start selling, and as soon as you start selling, you are in the sales cycle and the prospect's natural reaction kicks in to avoid the trap of getting sold to, resulting in a premature end to the conversation. Also keep in mind that we are talking about B2B space where the sales process, products, and services are often more expensive and complex. Therefore, you may need to do some research and properly prepare yourself for that first meeting.

Ingredients of a good appointment: ASK

When asking for an appointment, keep these guidelines in mind:

- Keep it brief
- Be all ears
- Be specific about follow-up
- Use your Winning Formula
- Stop Talking

Keep it Brief

Ask for ten to fifteen minutes for your first meeting. Don't ask for thirty minutes or an hour for your first call because more than likely won't get it. The most valuable asset of a manager or executive is time, and they don't part with it easily. Ask yourself how easy it is for you to get an appointment with your own company CFO or CEO or owner? Oftentimes not so easy. So don't expect an executive you spoke with for just two minutes to allocate a lot of time to you at this stage. It is hard to schedule an hour meeting at short notice without having to move a bunch of other appointments around. You don't want to make the experience of talking with you so difficult and painful.

Be All Ears

Remember, the first call is for listening to the prospect and seeing if there is much in common to continue talking. Don't start pitching on that short meeting. If you do, don't be surprised if you get shut down or get transferred to a department or person much lower in the organization who cannot give you budget.

There is certainly a good way and bad way to run your first meeting and this is also a big topic that I cover in my sales boot camps and opportunity management workshops.

Be Specific About Follow-Up

Give them a specific time and date for the appointment. Don't just leave it open for them to decide because it will become complicated and make them question the whole appointment. Often the sales executives attending my session say they worry that the executive may be busy the time they recommend and that is why they let the prospect decide the time. I agree that a schedule conflict may happen, but experience has shown that executives have no problem telling you the date you suggested doesn't work and offer you an alternative (if your Grabber was interesting enough). They have become executives because they can make decisions and not wallow in indecision

Don't make the appointment too close to your call. For example, don't call a CFO and say you want to talk with him tomorrow, unless they suggest it. I have called on 'C' level often, and more often than not, they gave me a date about two to four weeks later. They don't have so much free time.

Use Your *Winning Formula*

Don't ask for permission by phrases like, *"Do you have time next week...?"* Be more confident and to the point and ask for what you want; here are a few complete (Intro + Grabber + CTA) Winning Formula examples:

> *We work with VPs of sales to increase sales pipeline by up to 78%. I'd like fifteen minutes of your time next week on Friday at 2:00 p.m. to show you how we could help you.*

> *Hello, we helped XYZ retailer reduce internal theft and wastage by 80% and gross profit by 4%. I'd like fifteen minutes of your time next Thursday at 2:00 p.m. to see if we could help you achieve these kind of results.*

> *We help finance managers to improve Days Sales Outstanding by 14%. How about ten minutes of your time on Friday next week at 3:00 p.m. to discuss how we could help you?*

Stop Talking

Ask with confidence and be silent. Once you ask, let the silence hang in the air and don't say anything until they respond. Then go from there.

What Happens If?

One of the most immediate questions that comes up when I introduce the technique is, "But what if the person is not there?" or "What if the person is the wrong person to talk to?"

The answer is pretty simple. In case you don't know who the right person is, or you don't find the right person that would benefit from your products and services, then you have to find the right person. The best, fastest, easiest way to find the right person is to just ask the person you are contacting who would be the right person to talk to. By just asking the person who would be the best person who would care about your service you have the chance to identify a new contact and a potential prospect that is referred to you by someone in the prospect's company. I have found that asking to be referred to someone else in the prospect's company is easier than asking for an appointment because it takes almost no effort (if you ask properly) for the person to give someone's name and move on. So use this tool effectively and you will see great results.

Keep in mind that a contact name given to you by someone at the executive or 'C' level has a lot more power than getting someone's name from the receptionist or someone lower in the organization. As the old saying goes "It's not about what you know, it's about WHO you know." When you tell someone that your boss or someone at high level in your company gave me your name (referral) then you are more likely to get a warm reception. You don't want to start from low level and try to crawl your way to the top, because as we all know, there is a lot harder climbing uphill. When you get a referral from higher up in the company, you are more likely to be taken seriously than a referral from the bottom of the organization. As I mentioned, I find referrals sometimes much easier and better than asking for an appointment. Here is why:

- Easier to give a name than their own time for meeting.

- When you go to the top of the org. chart and get a referral, it is very likely that the person will agree to meet since his/her superior made the recommendation. I have had personal experience that I reached out to the CFO of a relatively large organization and asked for a referral. Once I called those referrals and told them that their manager told me to contact them, they became readily available to meet and spent a lot of time with me to scope out the company needs.

Prospecting via email or social media

The Grabber portion of your winning pitch will be the subject/title line and the first one or two sentences in your message. However, with email you can separate the function of the subject line and the first part of the message, with subject line getting the Attention (**A**IDA), and the first one or two sentences of the message to get the Interest (A**I**DA).

One of the best ways to get someone's attention is to talk about them. That is why the subject/title line of your sales prospecting email has to be about them and not you. I would actually use this technique even if I am trying to get someone's attention within my company. I would start the subject line by saying the department's name or start by saying, "*Your...*". Here are a few examples of how your subject/title lines could start:

"Your growth plan in 2016"

"Finance department's access to reports"

"Your posting on LinkedIn"

"Your industry trend in..."

"You will benefit from..."

Ask for an Appointment

For your 'ask' in a prospecting email, the options are the same; you ask for an appointment, and if you are not sure who is the right person you, ask to be referred to someone in the company.

One technique I found useful in asking an email prospect for appointment is to use my WP as a calendar invite and send it to the prospect. On a number of occasions, the prospect just replied by accepting and attended the meeting.

Multiple Touches

As I discussed in chapter 3, a key element of the Winning Formula technique is to reach your prospect with multiple touches before you give up. Your touches should include call, email and social media, with each touch being a little different. In case of email and social media, you could have couple of different subject/title lines and perhaps rewording your Grabber a bit.

Keep it Brief

The thirty-second rule applies to email as well. The reader should get through your WP within fifteen to thirty seconds. One of the benefits of email prospecting is that you could say a lot and put all kinds of data inside with links, images and stories. However, sending out long prospecting emails is not a good idea. I promise you that most people will not take the time to read through a prospecting email that came from a salesperson they don't know. The longer your prospecting message, the less likely it will be read. Keep your WP short.

 Make sure that your Winning Pitch is mobile-friendly as well. The reader should be able see your whole message in just one scroll/swipe on a smartphone. The reader should not be sliding multiple times to get to your point. So test your message first. Send it to your phone and make sure you could see the whole message in one scroll or swipe.

 Make sure you select a font size that is large enough and easily legible. Avoid fancy fonts that sometimes are not easy to read, especially on cell phones.

The number of sales calls it takes to close a sale is determined more by your own belief system than by the customer's willingness to buy.

CHAPTER 10 — THE WINNING FORMULA BEST PRACTICES

One of the questions you may be already asking is, "How often do I reach out to the prospect, and when is the best time for me to use the Winning Formula?" These are very important questions, and following these best practices will dramatically increase your success rate.

HOW OFTEN SHOULD YOU REACH OUT

An important ingredient of the Winning Formula technique is that you have to reach out to each of your prospects with multiple unique touches within a month; basically around one unique touch a week for 4 or 5 weeks. I use the word 'touch' because you should not limit yourself to a single method of contacting your prospect. You should use phone, email and social media at the minimum. This could be a phone call for the first touch, a LinkedIn InMail for the second touch, a Twitter direct message for the third touch, and so on. Here is a sample schedule:

MUST
- 1ˢᵗ touch, Tuesday - phone call
- 2²ᵈ touch, following Wednesday- LinkedIn InMail
- 3ʳᵈ touch, a few days later –Twitter message
- 4ᵗʰ touch, a week later– phone call

OPTIONAL
- 5ᵗʰ touch, a week later – email
- 6ᵗʰ touch, a week later – Share an article or customer success story

You may ask, "Do I create a new Winning Pitch for each of these touches?" The answer is 'No', you don't need to create a completely a new WP for each touch. Of course, you need to adjust your WP to the channel you are using since email has subject line, but you don't need that when you call. Twitter for example has a 140-character limit for your message so you may have to edit your WP for Twitter.

I want to add that you should try to make each touch a little different if you are using the same delivery channel. For example, if two of your four touches are emails, make the subject line a little different. Don't just send the same email four times. That's just being lazy and does not show a lot of customer focus when are spamming your prospects. What you should do is make minor changes such as changing the subject line a bit if you are sending multiple touches via email.

Don't use the same channel to do all your touches. People have different habits and work differently. I have seen some people who check email almost every ten minutes and check their LinkedIn once in a blue moon or only when they are looking for a job. I also have seen people that have their Twitter or Facebook open all the time and check email only at work. Using different channels gives you a higher chance of visibility and allows more flexibility for your prospects to choose their preferred method of engaging with you.

Best times to contact your prospects

This is another area where I find most sales executives are hurting themselves in their sales prospecting efforts. Again, you want to stay outside the sales cycle and don't make the prospect see you as another spammer or cold caller who calls the executive in the middle of the working day to push products. Do the unexpected. Contact them when they expect it the least, not during business hours! It would make perfect sense to try to contact prospects during the business hours because that is when they will be at work, right? Actually no, the normal business hours are the worst time to reach out to top managers and executives. Here is why: Consider what is the primary job of a company executive during the normal business hours? Take care of their business and people. They are having meetings, sending and receiving hundreds of messages to and from people that they know and have to deal with. They have no time to engage with strangers who want to ask for their money during business hours.

You will never find a blocked time in an executive's calendar for receiving cold calls. If you try to reach an executive who does not know you during the business hours, you are fighting against tremendous powers and will not get much traction. Your messages are unlikely to be noticed or looked at because they will be buried under hundreds of more important (from the prospect's point of view) messages. Plus, don't forget that the gatekeepers often scan the boss's emails and calls during the normal business hours and filter out anything that smells like a sales effort.

The best time to reach your executive prospects is before and after business hours and on the weekends, because these are about the only times that an executive can get his/her head above water and try to catch up with work. Don't forget that during off business hours, the gatekeepers are not there to block you. So you send an email, Twitter or LinkedIn InMail to the executive and allow them a few days to respond. If not, you just continue with your next touch a week or so later, and so on until you get through four or five touches discussed earlier. With emails that is easier because you can schedule the email to go out at a certain time automatically. Microsoft Outlook has that functionality.

Keep in mind that based on your target job title or industry or region you may have to adjust the number and type of touches. For example, in many Asian markets the face to face approach is still preferred by the prospects in some sectors. Therefore, you may have to do prospect visits more often than in other markets.

Why Does the Winning Formula Work?

As I discussed in Chapter 7, with the Winning Formula you improve your chances of success in prospecting by as much 500%. You may feel that this is a hoax and just not possible. After doing this for years, I have come up with 10 reasons why this technique is so effective:

1. It is simple and easy to learn. After just a couple of days of practice, you can build your Winning Pitches in minutes and seconds.

2. The Winning Formula is about the customer and not the vendor. This makes the messaging more impactful for the prospect.

3. You don't need to do a lot of research about the company to come up with a Winning Pitch.

4. The Winning Formula takes a lot of brain processing and decision making out of the prospect's hands and makes it easy for them to agree without thinking a great deal. In my opinion one of the reasons the traditional sales processing fails is that it requires the prospect to process a lot of unfamiliar information about the vendor's products and then make decisions based on the sales executive's questions. So it is easier for the prospect to just say 'No' at the beginning and move on.

5. Since the Winning Formula is different from the traditional prospecting style, it takes the prospect by surprise, and their traditional auto defense objections such as "don't need", "no money", "no sales calls allowed" don't get triggered, allowing you to have the prospect's attention long enough to land your Grabber and identify potential opportunities.

6. With the Winning Formula you are doing your best to avoid falling into the sales process by not selling.

You are just asking permission for a short dialog that is less threatening than a traditional sales call.

7. It lasts as little as a minute so the prospect does not feel like he/she is wasting a lot of time.

8. The direct approach of asking for what you want makes it easy for the prospect to avoid too much information processing. You are basically leading them to water without letting them worry about what to do.

9. With the Winning Formula you are engaging with the executives who have the power to say 'YES' to allocating budget for you if they see value in it. By starting at the top you are saving a great deal of time and resource in qualifying the opportunity right from the start.

10. The higher success rate of the Winning Formula technique will feed itself by making the sales executives more motivated and positive since they get much higher return on their effort and receive less rejections.

"Taking orders from customers who contact you is not selling. I call that customer service."

CHAPTER 11 — HANDLING COMMON CHALLENGES IN SALES PROSPECTING

Regardless of how good your Winning Pitch is, you will hear NO's and other objections that you need to deal with. Don't forget, with the Winning Formula a majority of your prospects will still say NO. I have put together a list of common objections and push-backs you may get from your prospects, along with suggestions on how to handle them.

But keep in mind that there are many ways to respond to an objection and there is no single 'right' way to do it. Every day I hear or read new tips and tricks on how to deal with different sales scenarios. The best way to keep everyone up to date is to share with you the latest updates through our online resources. Don't forget to visit the web page below for new ideas, tips, blogs, shares, tricks and tools that will help you be more successful.

(www.thewinningformulabook.com/resources)

#1- Prospect's response to your Winning Pitch: "Not interested."

What to do

Make sure the prospect is an executive holding the KPI that you cover in your WP. If so, and they genuinely don't have interest in your value proposition (reduce cost, improve revenue, increase market share, etc.) try to identify the reason why and if they could be a candidate for future contact.

I would still use social media to look up the individual and learn more about him/her to better identify the priorities. I would want to add them to my lead list in LinkedIn so that I am kept up-to-date on any updates and shares and look for any actionable insight that I could use for future contact.

#2- Prospect's response to your Winning Pitch: "Send us some information and we'll call you if interested."

What to do

First I would still insist that I need the email for the right executive (the one affected by the KPI in my WP) so that the message gets to the right person. I would go ahead and create a calendar invite for a fifteen-minute meeting at an appropriate future date and include my Winning Pitch in the invite and send to the right person.

In some cases, you may not get the email address of the right person as some companies have stricter policies on sharing employee information. In such cases I would want to at least know the executive's name that I could look up in social media and make a direct connection and reach them with my WP message.

If you are confident that you have delivered your WP effectively and the prospect sends a message or tells you 'not interested', I would make sure that the KPI in my WP is aligned with that role/person. I would try to reach other executives in the company that hold the KPI's effected by my solution.

#3- Prospect's response to your WP: "I have no time."

What to do:

Try to pick a date further out that will work with their schedule. As I discussed this before, most executives will not have free time to engage a salesperson immediately. You may have to go two to four weeks out in order to find a suitable date. If they are still unavailable but still seem to be interested in your WP, I would ask for the name of another executive that is also aligned to my WP's KPI and follow up with that person.

#4- Prospect's response to your WP: "Is this a sales call?"

What to do:

This is a common question coming from the receptionists or gatekeepers. There are a few ways to handle this one that I share with you.

Approach 1 — I say "No" and I repeat my WP, asking that I want to secure ten to fifteen minutes of the executive's time to discuss this as this is a business discussion that needs to take place with the executive you are seeking. In some scenarios when you are talking to a gatekeeper, especially one with a long history in that company, they can direct you to another executive-level person who may be interested in engaging with you. With this approach, sometimes I have explained that I have industry background and I am contacting the executive to share relevant industry information that would be of interest to the executive.

Approach 2 — First I want to explain a social phenomenon that should not be a surprise to you. People usually associate themselves with others in their social, professional, and economic class. What that means is that CEOs often hang out with CEOs, doctors with doctors, and celebrities with celebrities. You should use this desire to your advantage in prospecting. When seeking an engagement with an executive and coming across resistance to allow you in, explain to the gatekeeper that you were tasked by your CFO or VP to reach out to the prospect's CFO/CEO or VP of sales/marketing to set up a time for further discussion on improving business outcome (your WP value).

#5- Prospect's response to your WP: "We have no budget."

What to do:

First I would check and see if I am talking to the right job title. If I am, I would want to assure them that you are not seeking to sell anything. You are only asking for ten to fifteen minutes to see if you can help the company in achieving XYZ objective. After the short discussion, if the prospect does not see the value, then absolutely no obligation. The gain for the prospect is to talk with a subject matter expert who could offer some fresh ideas to help the prospect.

#6- Prospect's response to your WP: "I have five minutes, tell me more."

What to do:

This is a serious temptation for the salespeople because they are trained to jump on any opportunity to tell their story to anyone who wants to listen. When a prospect offers to give you five minutes, that is like asking a kid if he wants ice cream now vs. next week. Unfortunately, these scenarios usually don't end well. What often happens is that the salesperson starts to pitch for his/her company or product and it becomes a sales call. By this point the prospect has heard everything he wants to hear, and he just shuts you down or asks for price and then complains that your price is too high, etc. and then you are more than likely shut down.

What I suggest is to ask yourself can you really know enough about your prospect in a few minutes and is your product simple enough to be able to show the BUSINESS value in couple of minutes? In almost all cases the answer to the above questions is NO. If so then you should not take the bait.

The fact is, that in the case of B2B selling, especially for more complex organizations and products, you cannot possibly be ready to have that meeting there and then. You are not prepared and neither is your prospect. He is probably multitasking by checking emails reading documents or playing on his cell phone as he is allegedly listening to you. We all know how much attention span people have these days and the chance of them paying attention to a conversation that is not pre-planned.

The best practice here is to set up the meeting for some time in the future and explain to the prospect that you will be glad to listen to the prospect talk about his business, but it would be best to wait until the agreed-upon meeting time so that both parties are focused and ready to have that meeting. Don't forget that ten to fifteen-minute time you are asking for is not for you to pitch your products; it is for you to learn more about the client and if you could help them.

#7 Dealing with gatekeepers:

I know many sales people, both new and old timers, who hate to deal with gatekeepers. In many cases the sales executives are afraid of the gatekeepers and I have known reps who actually hang up the phone before saying a word as soon as they realize the gatekeeper has answered the phone. There are better ways to manage and leverage gatekeepers.

First let me explain what I mean by the word 'gatekeeper'. I use the term to refer to a person who acts as the firewall for the executive and protect him/her from wasting his/her most valuable possession, TIME. Often times the gatekeeper is given explicit instructions not to let any sales calls or sales executives to waste the executive's time. So the first factor you must keep in mind is that the gatekeeper's KPI is the complete opposite of yours; therefore, creating a key point of conflict in your relationship with the gatekeeper.

Important point to keep in mind is the difference between the gatekeeper and the receptionist. Don't confuse gatekeepers with the receptionists as they are different roles and have different KPIs. The receptionists are often there to just facilitate connecting the internal and external people via phone, digitally or in person. In bigger companies you will have these two roles with clear guidelines and KPIs. However, if you are calling smaller companies often times the gatekeeper and receptionist role may be handled by a single person.

Often times the receptionist's role is to route incoming calls, greet guests that visit the office, respond to emails and perform office related tasks. They often are not responsible for screening and qualifying every call before passing them to a desired person or department. As for the gatekeepers as mentioned before their job is often to protect the executives from distractions, with a major one being efforts of sales executives to get into the executive's office.

The reason I bring up the distinction between the two roles is that I have seen some sales executives do not distinguish between the two and end up hurting their cause by trying to explain the reason why they need to talk to someone in the company to a receptionist. Or they treat a gatekeeper like a receptionist and they are not ready for the gatekeeper asking a lot of questions to qualify the call before letting the conversation to take place.

Working with receptionists

When dealing with a receptionist at a prospect's site I recommend not spending too much time trying to explain the reason for your call or introducing yourself. I would just ask for the desired department or person (if I know the person). If I don't have a name to ask for, I ask for the relevant department such as finance or HR. Don't say any more than you have to.

Working with Gatekeepers

I have met many successful sale executive and I have found that they all have their own method of managing gatekeepers that works for them. Some sales executives have a friendlier and non-threatening approach and like to stay on the good side of the gatekeepers. These are the guys who remember the gatekeeper's important dates such as birthdays and maybe even send greeting cards or gifts on special occasions to the gatekeeper. I have seen other sales executives that try to avoid dealing with gatekeepers at all costs. There is some merit to either extreme approach. I like to share a few of the best practices I have seen that seem to work well for best of us.

Change your mindset

I read an interesting take on the role of the gatekeeper and I thought it makes a lot of sense. The writer was suggesting that when we label someone as a gatekeeper, we are mentally seeing that person as the enemy, trying to keep us out. Instead of calling the executive's assistant the 'gatekeeper' how about if we think of him/her as our 'sales assistant'? It may seem odd at first, but if you start to see the person as your sales assistant you will start to treat them differently and find a different approach to engage with them. Think about it and use it if you think it helps.

Treat them as the executive

I have met many executive assistants and gatekeepers who seem to be more powerful than the executives when it comes to knowing the company inside and out. Often times the gatekeepers (Sales assistants) can share insights that you will not get from the executives and they could refer you to the right people. So when it comes to delivering your Winning Pitch I strongly suggest delivering the exact same message to the gatekeeper and letting him/her to take the next step. You will be surprised at this approach's effectiveness.

The four magic words

Of the most effective techniques in working with the gatekeepers (sales assistants) is to use my favorite four-word question: *"Can you help me?"* You will be amazed how effective this question is when it comes to selling. But be careful how you use it. Because it is as powerful as a loaded gun and if you don't use it properly it will hurt you.

Now let me explain why I think it is such a powerful phrase. Let me ask you, if you are walking down the street and someone comes up to you and says the same magic phrase, "Can you help me?" what do you think you will say? I bet for almost 90%+ of you your reply will be something like "Yes, what do you need?" or "How can I help?" This is part of our DNA that when someone asks us for help our first reaction is *"How can I help?"* Basically you become attentive and try to help. When you say the four magic words to the gatekeeper (sales assistant) the person can become more attentive and listen to what you have to say without seeing you as a sales person. This provides you enough time to deliver your Winning Pitch (WP) and go for the call to action.

Now, you remember I said you have to use this weapon carefully? When you deliver this question to the prospect's gatekeeper (your sales assistant) you need to be silent after the question and let them respond to you. Don't keep talking and pitching. Because the person will stay in defensive posture and will be less likely to help you.

Just ask the question and be silent. Let them come back to you and ask you what you want. This is where you can deliver your WP.

Avoid normal business hours

As I mentioned in chapter ten, under the topic of "**Best times to contact your prospects**" I recommended that reaching for the executives during the business hours is not the best time to contact them. Since during the business hours the executives are focused on dealing with internal issues and dealing with day to day business, your call, email or social media message is likely to get lost in the mail box or get filtered out by the gatekeeper (sales assistant). The best way to avoid this filter is to reach the executive during the non-business hours which means outside of 9:00a.m. – 5:00pm time slot and on the weekends and holidays.

I personally have good level of success by calling 'C' level executives during the lunch break because often times the executives have a working lunch and the gatekeepers are away.

The point is that executives are so busy every day during the normal business hours that the only time they have to get caught up is after the normal business hours when the flow of internal and external calls and emails slows down.

By all means, this is not an exhaustive list, and I am sure there are many other scenarios that you come across. That is why we have taken this book and the important topic of demand generation to social media and have established multiple channels to keep our conversation going. We have established a number of forums online where you can share your thoughts, ideas, and expertise and learn from others professionals and experts.

CHAPTER 12 — EFFECTIVE SALES PROSPECTING THROUGH SOCIAL MEDIA

In my recently published book *Winning with Social Selling,* I shared how sales executives and organizations could best leverage various social channels to serve their markets better and become more successful. I also shared with my readers many success stories from across the globe where savvy organizations and sales executives are using the social media channels to better engage with their clients and generate more revenue. With over 50% of B2B buyers using social media in deciding what to buy, you cannot ignore this powerful opportunity generation tool.

Your Winning Social Channels

When it comes to B2B space for most of the major markets, you need to focus on LinkedIn and Twitter as your primary channels.

Keep in mind that in some markets such as Japan, China, and South Korea, LinkedIn does not have a strong base. Interestingly Facebook is popular in some countries, including Japan, as a viable B2B sales and marketing tool.

As many of you know, LinkedIn has a free membership version with limited functionality. However, if you are in the B2B space you should consider signing up for LinkedIn's social selling solution, the Sales Navigator. With the Sales Navigator you have a host of functions, including the ability to filter the 400-plus-million member database and set up alerts and save individuals as leads. I have supported a lot of sales and demand generation teams, and I am a believer that to be an effective social seller in the B2B space, you need to use LinkedIn's Sales Navigator that allows you to more effectively filter out and market to your target audience.

Twitter provides you with a very fast, mobile-friendly, and easy-to-use tool that will allow you to reach out to your target market, follow key thought leaders, and start one-on-one engagements. Twitter's 140-character limit will help you be more focused and cut out a lot of unnecessary wording.

Prospecting via social media

I have seen hundreds of sales executives use the social media a thousand ways to generate business. But there are mainly two approaches to the task. You can prospect via social media either through

1. Referrals, or
2. Insight

Prospecting via referral

Using referrals to find more customers is nothing new, and it is one of the most effective ways to find new business. Most sales executives highly under-utilize this approach, but that is a topic for another book. This is when you ask someone you know or have done business with to refer you to their friends or associates who may also benefit from your products and services.

With social media you have virtually unlimited scalability in getting new clients through your existing relationships. In the traditional selling model, you may have had a client refer you to his/her associate across the street or across town. But a referral through social media could come from someone thousands of miles away. I have been contacted by companies in multiple countries based on the feedback and testimonials I had received from a client in yet another country.

In seeking a referral or testimonial, you reach out to your existing clients, colleagues, and people you are connected with and ask for introduction to a third party. Social platforms such as LinkedIn have built-in forms and processes for seeking introductions and seeking testimonials.

LinkedIn allows you to get introductions to people through your existing connections. Another powerful function in LinkedIn is TeamLink which allows you to see if someone in your company is connected with a prospect. The logic here is that it is usually easier to ask someone in your company to introduce you to a third party.

A good approach I have seen with many successful sales executives is to search for the job title and/or companies they are targeting and then look up the individuals. If they have a person in their network that could do the introduction, then they send a message and ask for an introduction. In asking for an introduction, it is good etiquette to give them a way out in case they don't know that person well enough.

Prospecting via Showing Insight:

This is about showing your value to the target audience and earning the right to approach them, or better yet, get them to approach you. This could happen in two ways:

Outbound

Where you use your Winning Pitch in your message that you will direct to individuals or groups. For example, you put your WP (Winning Pitch) in a LinkedIn InMail and send to some of the executives that you know would benefit from your products and services. You may also post your WP on some relevant groups on LinkedIn, for example, telling the manufacturing CFOs group how you can help them improve DSO (Days Sales Outstanding). Or you may put your message in a Tweet and direct it to an individual or multiple people.

The social media is one of the channels you use to reach out to your target audience. As discussed in chapter 10, you should touch your prospects via phone, email, and social media to allow for your prospect to choose the most suitable way to respond.

Inbound

Inbound approach is where you position yourself as a subject matter expert and advisor who can add value to your target industry, business, or individual. By doing so, you establish awareness in your prospect's mind that you are not just a sales executive, but someone who can add value to the executive's business. As you realize, this is a long-term approach and requires more time to establish yourself and get noticed by the right audience. If you stay relatively active on social media, it could take you three to six months to start to get noticed and establish a following. The results could be in the form of getting contacted for discussion, people following you on social channels, your content being re-tweeted, getting comments, or being asked for your input or participation in discussions or groups.

As mentioned earlier, this is a long-term approach and not a one-time event. Just like the way you build your career over many years and not a single act, becoming a thought leader and subject matter expert requires long-term planning and steady, consistent social media presence.

I have to tell you that the inbound approach is what you should be aiming for as you are taking tactical steps through outbound activities for faster results. Once you become recognized as the 'go-to' person on a particular topic and continue to be *visible* and *relevant,* you should have little reason to worry about where your next deal will come from.

But notice that I used the words "visible and relevant". By visibility I mean that you have to stay active on social media and use the social media channels that your target clients use. For example, if your clients are mostly Facebook or Instagram users, then that's where you need to be.

Remaining 'relevant' means that you have to stay ahead of the game and lead your prospects in your area of expertise. With business and technology changing so rapidly, you have to continue to learn and grow with the market and your target audience. This is the downside of living in such exciting times with virtually endless possibilities. You need to continually learn, adapt, and transform yourself.

Tools of the trade

There are plenty of tools out there to improve and accelerate your presence on social media. These tools, mostly online, allow you to aggregate your social channels into a single screen, centralizing and automating content sharing. They could also track your postings and report on their effectiveness. For example, HootSuite allows you to track who got your content and who re-shared your content. Buffer is another social media management tool I have used for integrating and centralizing what I do on different social platforms. Then there are services such as Clout and PeerIndex to help you identify key influencers in your space and who your target audience sees as thought leaders.

I spent a lot of time going through various tools of the trade in my book, *Winning with Social Selling*. I suggest taking a look there if you want to learn more about social media channels and how to build a successful social presence.

Ideas that Work

I cover these topics in-depth in my latest book with explanations, examples, and scenarios. However, I want to share with you some fundamental steps you should be taking now to ensure your success in leveraging the social media. I will also share a few tried and true ideas on how to build and deliver insight to your target audience.

First step in your social media journey is to build your online profile with your target clients' needs and desires in mind. You want to build a profile that showcases your value add and your character. This is your first and most important step in building your presence and your network.

Second step is to find every platform that allows you to listen to your target clients and helps you to better understand their challenges, needs and aspirations. Remember that in today's connected world, people are talking about you and your organization with or without you. Savvy companies are using tools like Twitter to listen to and steal unhappy clients from their competitors. I have had the experience of sharing my dissatisfaction with some vendors and receiving a message from the company asking me how they could help me.

Step three is for you to start interacting with the social channels, sharing your insight and adding value to your target audience. This is where you start to build your brand as a subject matter expert, customer advocate, and business advisor. You can post ideas, market trends, industry analysis, best practices, surveys, and provocative questions to get people talking. A number of sales professionals who attended my social selling workshops joined LinkedIn groups in their target markets and posted some questions such as, "What do you think about the ABC model of doing XYZ?" then other group members started to post their opinions and shared their own experiences. The sales executives wasted no time to review the profiles of people who had commented and reached out to the ones that may have interest in their services and stated a number of dialogs that led into opportunities and revenue. Another sale executive decided to ask a target group to fill in a three-question survey about her company's services and asked how her company could improve. The flood of responses led to service improvements and ideas for new services with the promise of additional revenue.

What I hope you are getting from my stories is that the possibilities are endless and only limited by your imagination and commitment for achieving more.

Give, Give, Give, then Ask

Today's customers are the most educated and empowered buyers in history. Often you have to earn their attention and time by giving some value and share something of importance to them before you could ask for commitment. Social media allows you to do this more cost-effectively, and at light speed.

Social media-savvy companies and sales organizations are using the ubiquity of the channel to identify target buyers anywhere and get their attention by offering something of value to build brand and business. In the case of an airline passenger who just missed his flight, this could be an offer for a seat on the next flight with the competitor airline. For an executive who is frustrated with lack of innovation in his/her company, this could be an article on how to attract a creative and innovative workforce. The point is that you all have a great deal of value to add to your clients. But you need to get out there on the social media channels that your clients are using and start to build your brand, listen, and engage. Only then will you be rewarded with their attention and their business.

CHAPTER 13 — USING THE WINNING FORMULA ACROSS APAC MAJOR MARKETS

I have been living and working in the Asia Pacific for the past seventeen years and have done business in twenty or so countries. I also have taught and executed my Winning Formula workshops globally. Whenever I run my workshops, the local sales executives cannot wait to tell me how their culture is unique and the Winning Formula does not work in their country. I often acknowledge their opinion and do my workshop pretty much unchanged. What is great is that the next day when I run my execution and coaching sessions, they are shocked when they see that the technique actually worked in their unique culture!

Don't misunderstand, I agree that big differences exist among different cultures, and some methods work better in some places than others. Societies are made up of complex mixture of history, geography, race, religion, economy, and many other variables. However, as humans, we share similar feelings, emotions, concerns, needs, and aspirations.

I remember when I attended a speech by an executive from Starbucks over twenty years ago in Tokyo just before they opened their first store in Japan. A concern was raised by someone in the audience that the Starbucks coffee and the whole cafe experience is one unique to North America and not very 'Japanese'. The Starbucks executive smiled and acknowledged the point, and he shared the feedback they had heard in Chicago when they started to move from the West Coast of the United States to the East. He said they heard very similar concerns in Chicago that they liked their coffee less bold and just black and the store concept and price point would not work in Chicago. He went on to say that they did not change a single thing in their product when they entered the market there. Needless to say, twenty years on and you find Starbucks on almost every corner in Tokyo and across Japan full of people, often drinking the same coffee that you and I buy in Seattle.

The Winning Formula has been effective across multiple countries because it builds on similarities in the way we think, work, and make decisions. My technique's focus is on what the executive gets paid to care about, doesn't matter in which country. I acknowledge that the head of HR in Japan will probably do things very differently than the head of HR in New York. However, they are both responsible for attracting and retaining the best talents in the market. If you could show the HR head in Tokyo, New York, or Kuala Lumpur how you could help them recruit better talent, I assure you they will all be interested in talking with you regardless of the country they operate in.

I had a perfect proof point of this, in perhaps one of the most traditional major markets, Japan.

> *I was coaching a rep in connecting to the executive. All of the sales organizations and executives I have met in Japan are programmed to do the traditional personal and company introductions when calling on a prospect, which often could take a long time. Having lived, sold, and managed companies in Japan for ten years, I am very familiar with the process. In this case, the salesperson was determined to prove that the recommended system didn't work. But in the interest of progress, I agreed with him to do that, but make the introduction as short as possible and go right into the ask. So he called the CFO and delivered his Grabber. There was a short discussion about if and when he would have time, but at the end the prospect agreed to meet. After obtaining his email address and about to end the call, the prospect asked for the person's name and company name so he would look out for the message. Interestingly, this proved to the sales executive that the CFO did not really listen or care about his introduction at the start of the call. Only after he was interested in the message is when he asked for the salesperson's details.*

The Winning Formula technique has been perfected to avoid universally common negative brain triggers that often doom the sales prospecting efforts, such as sounding like a salesperson, asking questions such as, 'Do you have time?' or talking about products instead of the customer.

When I run my Winning Formula workshop in different countries, I adjust my formula a bit to accommodate local values and social etiquette. This is often around the introduction section of the formula as countries such as Japan, Korea, or China insist that it is inappropriate if you don't introduce yourself in full. I have to say that I have seen a good level of success without full self-introduction, even in the above countries. However, I don't want this to become a mental barrier for the sales executives to deal with, so I insist on a short and crisp self-introduction.

It is safe to say that in most Asian countries, it is expected to have an introduction. But you could make it very short and to the point. However, I strongly encourage you to take out any words and phrases that would get you kicked down the food chain and categorize you prematurely.

The other part of the Winning Formula in which I do minor adjustment is during the coaching sessions that happen right after the Winning Formula workshop, and it is two to three days long depending on the team's needs. As I mentioned in the book introduction section, during coaching days I work closely with the reps and monitor their execution of the technique, provide advice, and run debriefing sessions that allow us to capture and share the learning. Sometimes when I am coaching in the APAC region, I need to provide more detailed feedback or longer coaching sessions.

It has been my observation that in any country or sales team, if the workshop attendees came in with an open mind and tried the technique as described, they experienced results on par with all other countries and sales teams. However, if they did not apply themselves nor gave the technique a chance, then there wasn't a great deal of improvement. But then again, that is the case with anything we do. As the saying goes, 'If you believe it works or if you believe it doesn't work, you are right!"

ABOUT THE AUTHOR

Mark Ghaderi is an international speaker, sales trainer, coach, social selling expert and author and an entrepreneur with extensive experience helping small companies and Fortune 500 companies to grow sales by finding overlooked opportunities and customizing their sales process to be more effective at serving their clients.

With over seventeen years of living and working in the most dynamic and vibrant region of the world, Mark has traveled, lived in, & done business in all major Asian markets, with solid understanding and appreciation of the region's unique social and cultural values. As a global subject matter expert Mark has worked with dozens of organizations and thousands of sales professionals who are

looking for ways to improve their performance, better serve clients, and achieve personal and professional growth.

Having built and driven dozens of highly effective sales transformational initiatives, sales boot camps and Winner's Path sales workshops across multiple countries Mark possesses a rich, deep and practical approach to help individuals and companies to succeed through leveraging the enormous business and personal networks across ever growing social medial channels.

Mark lives and works in Singapore, operating throughout the Asia, EMEA and N. America markets.

ALSO BY MARK

Winning with Social Selling will help you leverage social media to build and maintain deeper client relationships and move from being just another vendor, to becoming a business partner.

Read more at:
www.winningwithsocialselling.com